Other books in this series:
Thank Heavens for Friends   For My Father
To My Grandmother with Love   Love a Celebration
For Mother a Gift of Love

EDITED BY HELEN EXLEY
BORDERS BY SHARON BASSIN

Published simultaneously in 1993 by Exley Publications in
Great Britain, and Exley Giftbooks in the USA.
Reprinted 1995.

Picture and text selection by © Helen Exley 1993.
Border Illustrations © Sharon Bassin 1993.

ISBN 1-85015-464-3

A copy of the CIP data is available from the British Library
on request.

Designed by Pinpoint Design.
Picture research by P. A. Goldberg and J. Clift / Image
Select, London.
Typeset by Delta, Watford.
Printed and bound by Grafo, S.A., Bilbao, Spain.

Exley Publications Ltd, 16 Chalk Hill, Watford,
Herts WD1 4BN, United Kingdom.
Exley Giftbooks, 232 Madison Avenue, Suite 1206, NY 10016, USA.

Picture Credits: AKG: page 18, 22, 26, 28, 38, 43, 45 © Willi Balendat (1901-
1969), "Epenstein platz, Reinickendorf", 1968. Rangendingen, Sammlung Klaus
Balendat, 51, 61. Chris Beetles: pages 25, 33, 57. Bridgeman Art Library: cover
and pages 6, 11, 14, 16 © Giovanni Battista-Crema, "Prisoners of the Mountain
Mists", 21 © Otto Muller (1874-1930) "The Gypsy Lovers", 30 Giraudon, 35 Fritz
Thaulow, 37, 40, 48 Index, 53, 55 © Manuel Lopes de Villasenor (b.1924), 58. City
of Bristol Museum & Art Gallery: page 37. Connaught Brown, London: page 35.
Museo Egiziano, Turnin: page 43. Museo Cau Ferrat, Sitges, Catalonia: page 48.
Fine Art Photographic Library Ltd: page 9, 13, 34. Giraudon: title page and page
46. Van der Heydt Museum, Wuppertal: page 38. Collection Max Lutze,
Hamburg: page 21. Musees des Beaux Arts, Lyon: page 22. Roy Miles Gallery,
London: page 40. Nationalgalerie SMPK, Berlin: page 61. Magyar Nemzeti
Galeria, Budapest: page 6. Musee Beaux Arts, Tournai: page 46.Musee d'Orsay,
Paris: pages 28, 30. Whitford & Hughes, London: page 16.

Marriage

A KEEPSAKE

EDITED BY
HELEN EXLEY

EXLEY
NEW YORK • WATFORD, UK

GIFT OF SIGHT

I had long known the diverse tastes of the wood,
Each leaf, each bark, rank earth from every
  hollow;
Knew the smells of bird's breath and of bat's
  wing;
Yet sight I lacked: until you stole upon me,
Touching my eyelids with light finger-tips.
The trees blazed out, their colours whirled
  together,
Nor ever before had I been aware of sky.

ROBERT GRAVES

ROMANCE

I will make you brooches and toys for your
    delight
Of bird-song at morning and star-shine at night.
I will make a palace, fit for you and me,
Of green days in forests, and blue days at sea.

I will make my kitchen, and you shall keep your
    room,
Where white flows the river and bright blows
    the broom,
And you shall wash your linen and keep your
    body white
In rainfall at morning and dewfall at night.

And this shall be for music when no one else is
    near,
The fine song for singing, the rare song to hear!
That only I remember, that only you admire,
Of the broad road that stretches and the
    roadside fire.

ROBERT LOUIS STEVENSON

A SLICE OF WEDDING CAKE

Why have such scores of lovely, gifted girls
　　Married impossible men?
Simple self-sacrifice may be ruled out,
　　And missionary endeavour, nine times
　　　　out of ten.

Repeat "impossible men": not merely rustic,
　　Foul-tempered or depraved
(Dramatic foils chosen to show the world
　　How well women behave, and always have
　　　　behaved).

Impossible men: idle, illiterate,
　　Self-pitying, dirty, sly,
For whose appearance even in City parks
　　Excuses must be made to casual passers-by.

Has God's supply of tolerable husbands
　　Fallen, in fact, so low?
Or do I always over-value woman
　　At the expense of man?
　　　　　　Do I?
　　　　　　　　It might be so.

ROBERT GRAVES

EPITHALAMION

Singing, today I married my white girl
beautiful in a barley field.
Green on thy finger a grass blade curled,
so with this ring I thee wed, I thee wed,
and send our love to the loveless world
of all the living and all the dead.

Now, no more than vulnerable human,
we, more than one, less than two,
are nearly ourselves in a barley field -
and only love is the rent that's due
though the bailiffs of time return anew
to all the living but not the dead.

Shipwrecked, the sun sinks down harbours
of a sky, unloads its liquid cargoes
of marigolds, and I and my white girl
lie still in the barley - who else wishes
to speak, what more can be said
by all the living against all the dead?

Come then all you wedding guests:
green ghost of trees, gold of barley,
and blackbird priests in the field,
you wind that shakes the pansy head
fluttering on a stalk like a butterfly;
come the living and come the dead.

Listen flowers, birds, winds, worlds,
tell all today that I married
more than a white girl in the barley -
for today I took to my human bed
flower and bird and wind and world,
and all the living and all the dead.

DANNIE ABSE

i carry your heart with me (i carry it in
my heart) i am never without it (anywhere
i go you go, my dear; and whatever is done
by only me is your doing, my darling)
                                        i fear
no fate (for you are my fate, my sweet) i want
no world (for beautiful you are my world, my
    true)
and it's you are whatever a moon has always
    meant
and whatever a sun will always sing is you

here is the deepest secret nobody knows
(here is the root of the root and the bud of the
    bud
and the sky of the sky of a tree called life; which
    grows
higher than soul can hope or mind can hide)
and this is the wonder that's keeping the stars
    apart

i carry your heart (i carry it in my heart)

E.E. CUMMINGS

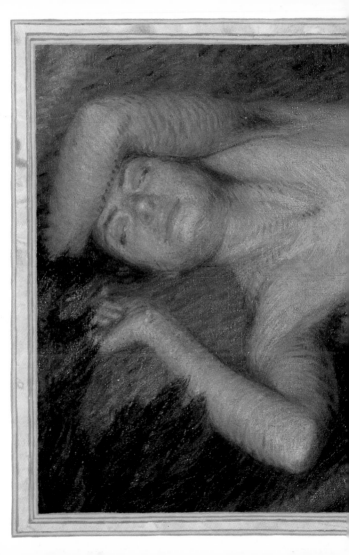

Desire
has tied my hands
and love
has given me to you
as a slave
a willing
   meek
   docile
   abject
slave
who will never ask for
bitter freedom.

RUFINOS

Antonio, that good fellow,
has recently got married
and is happy with his wife,
for there is no one lovelier,
sweeter, and more faithful,
more filled with affection,
more free of duplicity,
gentler of character,
easier to seduce -

RUBEN DARIO

THE AUTHOR TO HIS WIFE, OF A WOMAN'S ELOQUENCE

My Mall, I mark that when you mean to
   prove me
To buy a velvet gown, or some rich border,
Thou call'st me good sweet heart, thou swear'st
   to love me,
Thy locks, thy lips, thy looks, speak all in order,
Thou think'st, and right thou think'st, that
   these do move me,
That all these severally thy suit do further:
   But shall I tell thee what most thy suit
     advances?
   Thy fair smooth words? no, no, thy fair
    smooth haunches.

Sir John Harington

MR. EDWARDS: Myfanwy Price!

MISS PRICE: Mr. Mog Edwards!

MR. EDWARDS: I am a draper mad with love. I love you more than all the flannelette and calico, candlewick, dimity, crash and merino, tussore, cretonne, crepon, muslin, poplin, ticking and twill in the whole Cloth Hall of the world. I have come to take you away to my Emporium on the hill, where the change hums on wires. Throw away your little bedsocks and your Welsh wool knitted jacket, I will warm the sheets like an electric toaster, I will lie by your side like the Sunday roast.

MISS PRICE: I will knit you a wallet of forget-me-not blue, for the money to be comfy. I will warm your heart by the fire so that you can slip it in under your vest when the shop is closed.

MR. EDWARDS: Myfanwy, Myfanwy, before the mice gnaw at your bottom drawer will you say.

MISS PRICE: Yes, Mog, yes, Mog, yes, yes, yes.

MR. EDWARDS: And all the bells of the tills of the town shall ring for our wedding.

DYLAN THOMAS

THAT'S ENOUGH FOR ME

If I can make you cry
If I can fill your eyes with pleasure
Just by holding you
In the early hours of mornin'
When the day that lies ahead's
Not quite begun

. . . If I can make you smile
If I can move you close
To laughter with a word or two
When your day's been filled with strangers
And the castles that you build
All tumble down

Oh well, that's enough for me
That's all the hero I need to be
I smile to think of you and me
You and I
And how our pleasure makes you cry

PAUL WILLIAMS

A LOVE POEM

——whose body has opened
Night after night
Harbouring loneliness,
Cancelling the doubts
Of which I am made,
Night after night
Taste me upon you.

Night and then again night,
And in your movements
The bed's shape is forgotten.
Sinking through it I follow,
Adrift on the taste of you.

I cannot speak clearly about you.
Night and then again night,
And after a night beside you
Night without you is barren.

I have never discovered
What alchemy makes
Your flesh different from the rest,
Nor why all that's commonplace
Comes to seem unique,

And though down my spine one answer leaks
It does not bother to explain itself.

BRIAN PATTEN

IN SEPTEMBER

Again the golden month, still
Favourite, is renewed;
Once more I'd wind it in a ring
About your finger, pledge myself
Again, my love, my shelter,
My good roof over me,
My strong wall against winter.

Be bread upon my table still
And red wine in my glass; be fire
Upon my hearth. Continue,
My true storm door, continue
To be sweet lock to my key;
Be wife to me, remain
The soft silk on my bed.

Be morning to my pillow,
Multiply my joy. Be my rare coin
For counting, my luck, my
Granary, my promising fair
Sky, my star, the meaning
Of my journey. Be, this year too,
My twelve months long desire.

JOHN ORMOND

CAN'T HELP LOVIN' DAT MAN

Mah man is shiftless
An' good fo' nothin' too,
He's mah man jes' de same.
He's never near me when dere is work
    to do.

. . . Fish got to swim and birds got to fly,
I got to love one man till I die,
Can't help lovin' dat man of mine.
Tell me he's lazy, tell me he's slow,
Tell me I'm crazy, maybe I know.
Can't help lovin' dat man of mine!

. . . When he goes away,
Dat's a rainy day,
An' when he comes back dat day is fine,
The sun will shine.
He can come home as late as can be,
Home without him ain't no home to me,
Can't help lovin' dat man of mine!

OSCAR HAMMERSTEIN 2ND

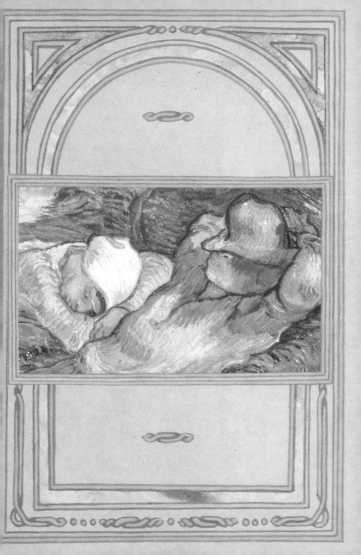

A SINGLE FLOWER

I can't talk to rocks
and trees, but I talk
to myself too much.
I'll grow a single flower
in my garden
and give it to my wife.
Is a man any less a poet
because he stays home
with his wife and children,
or is poetry always written
by someone wild?

This is not a poem
about marriage.
It's a poem about love.
I have lived with one woman
for nearly twelve years,
and although I only write
a short poem
each time we're together,
I also add a line
to a longer poem
for a later year.

JIM BURNS

QUIET SONG
IN TIME OF CHAOS

Here
Is home.
Is peace.
Is quiet.

Here
Is love
That sits by the hearth
And smiles into the fire,
As into a memory
Of happiness,
As into the eyes
Of quiet.

Here
Is faith
That can be silent.
It is not afraid of silence.
It knows happiness
Is a deep pool
Of quiet.

Here
Sadness, too,
Is quiet.
Is the earth's sadness
On autumn afternoons
When days grow short,
And the year grows old,
When frost is in the air,
And suddenly one notices
Time's hair
Has grown whiter.

Here?
Where is here?
But you understand.
In my heart
Within your heart
Is home.
Is peace.
Is quiet.

EUGENE O'NEILL,
TO CARLOTTA ON HER BIRTHDAY

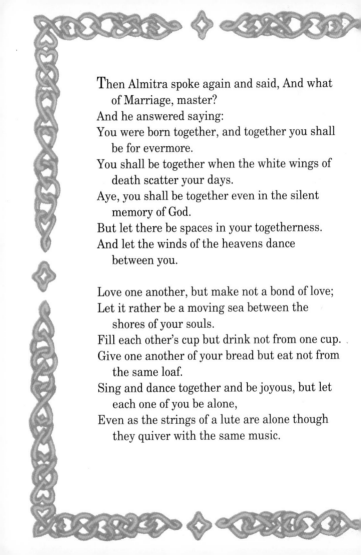

Then Almitra spoke again and said, And what of Marriage, master?

And he answered saying:

You were born together, and together you shall be for evermore.

You shall be together when the white wings of death scatter your days.

Aye, you shall be together even in the silent memory of God.

But let there be spaces in your togetherness.

And let the winds of the heavens dance between you.

Love one another, but make not a bond of love;

Let it rather be a moving sea between the shores of your souls.

Fill each other's cup but drink not from one cup.

Give one another of your bread but eat not from the same loaf.

Sing and dance together and be joyous, but let each one of you be alone,

Even as the strings of a lute are alone though they quiver with the same music.

Give your hearts, but not into each other's
    keeping.
For only the hand of Life can contain your
    hearts.
And stand together yet not too near together:
For the pillars of the temple stand apart,
And the oak tree and cypress grow not in each
    other's shadow.

KAHLIL GIBRAN, "THE PROPHET"

How wise I am to have instructed the butler to instruct
the first footman to instruct the second footman to
instruct the doorman to order my carriage;
I am about to volunteer a definition of marriage. Just
as I know that there are two Hagens, Walter and Copen,
I know that marriage is a legal and religious alliance
entered into by a man who can't sleep with the window
shut and a woman who can't sleep with the window open.
Moreover, just as I am unsure of the difference between
flora and fauna and flotsam and jetsam,
I am quite sure that marriage is the alliance of two
people one of whom never remembers birthdays and
the other never forgetsam,
And he refuses to believe there is a leak in the water
pipe or the gas pipe and she is convinced she is about to
asphyxiate or drown.
And she says Quick get up and get my hairbrushes off
the windowsill, it's raining in, and he replies Oh they're
all right, it's only raining straight down.
That is why marriage is so much more interesting than
divorce,
Because it's the only known example of the happy
meeting of the immovable object and the irresistible force.
So I hope husbands and wives will continue to debate
and combat over everything debatable and combatable,
Because I believe a little incompatibility is the spice of
life, particularly if he has income and she is pattable.

Ogden Nash, "I do, I will, I have"

TRUST

Oh we've got to trust
one another again
in some essentials.

Not the narrow little
bargaining trust
that says: I'm for you
if you'll be for me.

But a bigger trust,
a trust of the sun
that does not bother
about moth and rust,
and we see it shining
in one another.

Oh don't you trust me,
don't burden me
with your life and affairs;
  don't thrust me
into your cares.

But I think you may trust
the sun in me
that glows with just
as much glow as you see
in me, and no more.

But if it warms
your heart's quick core
why then trust it, it forms
one faithfulness more.

And be, oh be
a sun to me,
not a weary, insistent
personality

but a sun that shines
and goes dark, but shines
again and entwines
with the sunshine in me

till we both of us
are more glorious
and more sunny.

D. H. LAWRENCE

Love is something far more than desire for sexual intercourse; it is the principal means of escape from the loneliness which affects most men and women throughout the greater part of their lives. There is a deep-seated fear in most people, of the cold world and the possible cruelty of the herd; there is a longing for affection, which is often concealed by roughness, boorishness or a bullying manner in men, and by nagging and scolding in women. Passionate mutual love while it lasts puts an end to this feeling; it breaks down the hard walls of the ego, producing a new being composed of two in one. Nature did not construct human beings to stand alone, since they cannot fulfil her biological purpose except with the help of another; and civilized people cannot fully satisfy their sexual instinct without love. The instinct is not completely satisfied unless a man's whole being, mental quite as much as physical, enters into the relation. Those who have never known the deep intimacy and the intense companionship of mutual love have missed the best thing that life has to give; unconsciously, if not consciously, they feel this, and the resulting disappointment inclines them towards envy, oppression and cruelty. To give due place to passionate love should be therefore a matter which concerns the sociologist, since, if they miss this experience, men and women cannot attain their full stature, and cannot feel towards the rest of the world that kind of generous warmth without which their social activities are pretty sure to be harmful.

BERTRAND RUSSELL

Cuckoos lead Bohemian lives,
They fail as husbands and as wives,
Therefore they cynically disparage
Everybody else's marriage.

OGDEN NASH

In villages in Pakistan, a prospective bridegroom is brought before relatives of the bride, who insult him with every known invective. The theory is that, if he can take that, he has nothing to fear from what the bride will say later.

ROBIN RAY

Marriage is the best state for man in general; and every man is a worse man in proportion as he is unfit for the married state.

JOHNSON

Let me not to the marriage of true minds
Admit impediments. Love is not love
Which alters when it alteration finds,
Or bends with the remover to remove:
O, no! It is an ever fixed mark,
That looks on tempests and is never shaken,
It is the star to every wandering bark,
Whose worth's unknown, although his height be
    taken
Love's not Time's fool, though rosy lips and
    cheeks
Within his bending sickle's compass come;
Love alters not, with his brief hours and weeks,
But bears it out even to the edge of doom.
If this be error and upon me proved,
I never writ, nor no man ever loved.

WILLIAM SHAKESPEARE

THIS IS OUR PLACE

This bed is our island. Only the occasional cat shares our solitude. We listen to the voices of the sea, but pay no heed. We have shed the everyday. It sprawls forgotten on the chairs and floor. This is our place, our haven. Here we can rediscover one another, sleep in each other's arms. Here we can find ourselves again. The world tears at us. Sometimes we scarcely know if we exist outside its rough demands. Only here, only in each other's arms, we rediscover joy. Only here we are ourselves, and so each other's.

PAM BROWN

it may not always be so; and i say
that if your lips, which i have loved, should
 touch
another's, and your dear strong fingers clutch
his heart, as mine in time not far away;
if on another's face your sweet hair lay
in such a silence as i know, or such
great writhing words as, uttering overmuch,
stand helplessly before the spirit at bay;

if this should be, i say if this should be -
you of my heart, send me a little word;
that i may go unto him, and take his hands,
saying, Accept all happiness from me.
Then shall i turn my face, and hear one bird
sing terribly afar in the lost lands.

E.E. CUMMINGS

I am by nature conventional and straightforward, but Yün was a stickler for forms, like the Confucian schoolmasters. Whenever I put on a dress for her or tidied up her sleeves, she would say "So much obliged" again and again, and when I passed her a trowel or a fan, she must receive it standing up. At first I disliked this and said to her: "Do you mean to tie me down with all this ceremony? There is a proverb which says, 'One who is overcourteous is crafty.'" Yün blushed all over and said: "I am merely trying to be polite and respectful; why do you charge me with craftiness?" "True respect is in the heart, and does not require such empty forms," said I, but Yün said, "There is no more intimate relationship than that between children and their parents. Do you mean to say that children should behave freely towards their parents and keep their respect only in their heart?" "Oh! I was only joking," I said. "The trouble is," said Yün, "most marital troubles begin with joking. Don't you accuse me of disrespect later, for then I shall die of grief without being able to defend myself." Then I held her close to my breast and caressed her and then she smiled. From then on our conversations were full of "I'm sorry's" and "I beg your pardon's." And so we remained courteous to each other for twenty-three years of our married life like Liang Hung and Meng Kuang of old, and the longer we stayed together, the more passionately attached we became to each other. Whenever we met each other in the house, whether it be in a dark room or in a narrow corridor, we used to hold each other's hands and ask: "Where are you going?" and we did this on the sly as if afraid that people might see us. As a matter of fact, we tried at first to avoid being seen sitting or walking together, but after a while, we did not mind it any more. When Yün was sitting and talking with somebody and saw me come, she would rise and move sideways for me to sit down together with her. All this was done naturally almost without any consciousness, and although at first we felt uneasy about it, later on it became a matter of habit. I cannot  understand why all old couples must hate each other like enemies. Some people say "if they weren't enemies, they would not be able to live together until old age." Well, I wonder!

SHEN FU, EXTRACT FROM "WEDDED BLISS"

WHEN A BELOVED HAND

When a belovèd hand is laid in ours,
When, jaded with the rush and glare
Of the interminable hours,
Our eyes can in another's eyes read clear,
When our world-deafened ear
Is by the tones of a loved voice caressed, -
A bolt is shot back somewhere in our breast,
And a lost pulse of feeling stirs again.
The eye sinks inward, and the heart lies plain,
And what we mean, we say, and what we would,
   we know!
A man becomes aware of his life's flow,
And hears its winding murmur, and he sees
The meadows where it glides, the sun, the
   breeze.

And there arrives a lull in the hot race,
Wherein he doth for ever chase
That flying and elusive shadow, rest.

An air of coolness plays upon his face,
And an unwonted calm pervades his breast.
And then he thinks he knows
The hills where his life rose,
And the sea where it goes.

MATTHEW ARNOLD

WINSTON TO CLEMENTINE
CHURCHILL

You ought to trust me for I do not love and will never love any woman in the world but you, and my chief desire is to link myself to you week by week by bonds which shall ever become more intimate and profound. Beloved I kiss your memory - your sweetness and beauty have cast a glory upon my life. You will find me always

Your loving and
devoted husband W

WINSTON CHURCHILL

And man and woman are like the earth, that brings forth flowers
in summer, and love, but underneath is rock.
Older than flowers, older than ferns, older than foraminiferae
older than plasm altogether is the soul of a man underneath.

And when, throughout all the wild orgasms of love
slowly a gem forms, in the ancient, once-more-molten rocks
of two human hearts, two ancient rocks, a man's heart and a woman's,
that is the crystal of peace, the slow hard jewel of trust,
the sapphire of fidelity.
The gem of mutual peace emerging from the wild chaos of love.

D. H LAWRENCE, FROM "FIDELITY"

TOUCH

and no sound
and no word spoken
and the window pane
grey in dwindling light
and no word spoken
but touch, your touch
upon my hand veined
by the changing years
that gave and took away
yet gave a touch
that took away
the years between
and brought to this grey day
the brightness we had seen
before the years had grown between.

GEORGE BRUCE

Acknowledgements: The publishers gratefully acknowledge permission to reproduce copyright material, and would be intereted to hear from any copyright holders not here acknowledged.

DANNIE ABSE: "Epthalamion" from *Walking Under Water*. Reprinted by permission of Sheil Land Associates Ltd; GEORGE BRUCE: "Touch", from *Collected Poems*, Edinburgh University Press. Reprinted by permission of the author; JIM BURNS: "A Single Flower", reprinted with permission of the author; WINSTON CHURCHILL: "Letter to his wife", reprinted with permission of the Curtis Brown Group Ltd; E.E. CUMMINGS: "it may not always be so;and i say", reprinted from *Tulips & Chimneys* by permission of Liveright Publishing Corporation and W.W. Norton & Co. Ltd. Copyright © 1973, 1976 by Nancy T. Andrews © 1973, 1976 by George James Firmage; "i carry your heart with me(i carry it in", copyright 1952 by e.e. cummings. Reprinted from *Complete Poems 1913-1935* by permission of Liveright Publishing Corporation and *Complete Poems 1936-1962* by W.W. Norton & Co. Ltd. SHEN FU: Excerpt from *The Wisdom of China and India*, edited by Lin Yutang. Copyright 1942 and renewed 1970 by Random House Inc. Reprinted with permission of the publisher; KAHLIL GIBRAN: Extract from *The Prophet*, reprinted with permission of A.P. Knopf, a division of Random House Inc; ROBERT GRAVES: "A Slice of Wedding Cake" and "Gift of Sight" from *Collected Poems 1975*, reprinted with permission of A.P. Watt Ltd and the Trustees of the Robert Graves Copyright Trust and Oxford University Press, New York; OSCAR HAMMERSTEIN II: extract from "Can't Help Lovin' Dat Man" from *Showboat*, music by Jerome Kern. Copyright © 1927 by T.B. Harms Company copuright renewed. International copyright secured. Used by permission of T.B. Harms and Polygram Music; ADRIAN HENRI: extract from "Who" from *Collected Poems 1965-1985*, published by Allison & Busby 1986 © Adrian Henri 1986, reprinted with permission of Rogers, Coleridge and White Ltd; D.H. LAWRENCE: "Fidelity" and "Trust" from *The Complete Poems of D.H. Lawrence* © 1964, 1971 by Angelo Ravagli and C.M. Weekley, Executors of the Estate of Frieda Lawrence Ravagli. Used by permission of Viking Penguin, a division of Penguin Books USA Inc; OGDEN NASH: "I Do , I Will, I Have", first appeared in *The Saturday Evening Post*, from *Verses from 1929 On*. Copyright 1948, 1950 by Ogden Nash. Copyright © renewed 1975, 1987 by Frances Nash, Isabel Nash Eberstadt, and Linell Nash Smith. "The Cuckoo", first appeared in *The New Yorker*, from *Verses from 1929 On*, copyright 1953 Ogden Nash. Reprinted by permission of Little Brown & Company and Curtis Brown . EUGINE O'NEILL: "A Quiet Song in Time of Chaos", from *Poems 1912-1944*, edited by Donald Gallup, Copyright © 1979 by Yale University. Reprinted by permission of Ticknor & Field/Houghton Mifflin Co. and Random House UK Ltd and the Executors of the Eugene O' Neill Estate . All rights reserved. JOHN ORMOND: "In September", reprinted with permission of Glenys Ormond; BRIAN PATTEN: "A Love Poem" from *Love Poems (Vanishing Trick)*, published by George Allen & Unwin Ltd, now Unwin Hyman, and imprint of HarperCollins Publishers Ltd; ROBIN RAY: extract from *Time For Lovers*, published by Weidenfeld & Nicolson Ltd; BERTRAND RUSSELL: extract from "Marriage and Morals". © 1929 by Horace Liveright, copyright 1957 Bertrand Russell. Reprinted with permission of International Thomson Publishing Services Ltd and Liveright Publishing Corporation; GEORGE BERNARD SHAW: extract from *Man and Superman*. Reprinted with permission of The Society of Authors on behalf of the Bernard Shaw Estate; RAYMOND SOUSTER: "Not Wholly Lost", from *Collected Souster Volume 1*. Reprinted with permission of Oberon Press, Ottawa, Canada; DYLAN THOMAS: extract from *Under Milk Wood*, published by J.M. Dent. Reprinted with permlssion of David Higham Associates Ltd; PAUL WILLIAMS: "That's Enough For Me", reprinted by permission of Rondor Music (London) Ltd.